Reykjavik to Rome

Everton and Liverpool fans in Europe

Compiled and edited

by

Janet Goodwin and Len Straughan

First published 1996 by Picton Press.
1 & 3 Grove Road, Rock Ferry
Birkenhead, Wirral, Merseyside L42 3XS.

Picton Press - Liverpool is the joint publishing imprint of The City of Liverpool - Libraries & Information & Information Services. (part of the Leisure Directorate) & Countyvise Limited.

The City of Liverpool

ISBN 1 873245 05 X

Typeset & Printed by Birkenhead Press Limited
1 & 3 Grove Road, Rock Ferry
Birkenhead, Wirral, Merseyside L42 3XS.

Contents

Rotterdam

Rome

Tbilisi

Foreword

In the summer of 1996 the City of Liverpool played host to several of the games in the European Soccer Championship, the third largest sports event in the world. It was fitting that Liverpool should have been chosen to be one of the host centres as the city's two clubs have an unrivalled British record of success in the various European competitions, bringing each of the European club trophies to the city. The supporters of Liverpool and Everton have a special regard for the European ties, as they provide an opportunity to see many of Europe's finest teams and players perform on the hallowed turf of Goodison or Anfield. For many supporters the European club tournaments also offer a unique means of sharing their love for the people's game with supporters from all corners of the continent.

This collection of reminiscences is an attempt to capture and share those experiences. Some of the writers may well be familiar names to you, some probably not. But all the contributors share an authentic and deep love for the game and their teams. Here is a chance to feel the ecstatic highs and tragic lows that our supporters have witnessed and felt.

1

Early Days

When we started playing the European clubs in the 1960's and saw teams like Inter Milan, Benfica and Bayern Munich arriving in Liverpool...the clubs which only Manchester United had played, and to see them at Anfield, well, it was just brilliant.

It always seemed cold and wet though...misty. I remember the night of the "big steam" when there were 28,000 standing on the Kop. They had been out in the rain for two hours and when they got in their body heat just evaporated all the water so nobody could see. The whole Kop just pushed forward and they were sitting all round the pitch. It was chaos, but it was great, a really good time.

There was also the night - I think it was against Reykjavik in the European Cup - when we couldn't see the Anfield Road End because of the mist and you'd hear the crowd roar, "Goal!" and the Kop would chant, "Who scored?" The Road End would chant back a name and the Kop would return with, "How did they score?" and then they'd chant it was a header. There was always something going on, it didn't matter how boring the game was!

Professor Phil Redmond

Reykjavik to Rome • Reykjavik to Rome • Reykjavik to Rome • Reykjavik to Rome • Reykjavik to Rome •

2

Liverpool v Inter Milan

European Cup Semi-final
1st Leg 4th May 1965

Sitting in his bunker beneath the old wooden stand Bill Shankly could hear the thunderous roar above him. "Ee-Aye-Addio, We Wanna See Der Cup," rang the chorus around the ground. In the dressing rooms the players could barely hear themselves talk. For Inter Milan it must have been terrifying; for ten year old Phil Thompson on his first visit to Anfield it was to be the start of a love affair with the club; for sixteen year old Steve Kelly up on the Kop it was breathtaking. Years later when I came to write a book about the Kop I asked the inevitable question; what was your greatest memory? For anyone over the age of forty the answer was instant: Liverpool versus Inter Milan, semi-final of the European Cup, May 1965.

What made it so memorable was that a couple of days earlier Liverpool had won the FA Cup for the first time in their history. Evertonians used to wisecrack that the day Liverpool picked up the Cup the Liver Bird would fly off its perch at the Pier Head. That Saturday evening thousands of Scousers, much the worse for celebrating, had congregated at the Pier Head to see if the famous bird was still there. It was, though the next day, as Liverpool returned to the city clutching their prize, it might easily have fled in fear as almost a million people packed the city centre to greet their heroes.

4

That was on the Sunday. On the Tuesday evening there was only one place to be. I was a young apprentice at the time, busying away at the Cammell Laird shipyard in Birkenhead. Having missed Wembley I was desperate not to miss this one but it was clear that getting in was going to be near impossible. There were no tickets for the Kop; it was a case of first come, first served. And as I didn't finish work until 5.30pm, it was likely to be 6.30pm before I could reach Anfield.

"There's only one thing for it," announced fellow apprentice Pete over lunch, "I'm going to ask the boss for time off." We looked at him as if he had gone loopy. But he was determined and into Joe's office he strode. Five minutes later he re-emerged beaming. Now the thing about Joe was that he was a decent sort. He may not have been a football fan but like everyone else in Liverpool he had been caught up in the fervour. Bill was next in. "He's chancing his arm," I thought. But no, out he came rubbing his hands. "He says I can go at 4.00," he reported.

That was it. I was next in. "Oh Christ, not another," said Joe, barely glancing up from his drawing board. "I suppose you want time off as well. Bugger me. Well, if I've given it to one I suppose I have to let you go. Might as well close the bloody office down for the afternoon."

At 4.00pm the three of us were off, out of the gates, up the road and onto the underground. We arrived at Anfield just after 5.00pm. The gates hadn't been long open and already the queues were stretching two hundred yards down the road. We finally made it into the Kop not long after 5.30pm; half an hour later the doors of the Kop were slammed shut. For the next hour and a half there was little to do but sing. "Ee-Aye-Addio, We Wanna See Der Cup," we yelled til we were hoarse, followed by various derogatory chants at the small number of Italians in the Kemlyn Road stand. Most of it was to do with how we beat them in the War. Thirty years on I can't say that I'm particularly proud at what I was chanting. More memorably, to the tune of Santa Lucia we gloated, "Go back to It-al-ee, go back to It-al-ee."

Meanwhile Bill Shankly, hearing this deafening noise came up with a plan. Before the teams came out onto the pitch he would send the Cup out. That would frighten the

• Reykjavik to Rome • Reykjavik to Rome • Reykjavik to Rome • Reykjavik to Rome •

Italians. In fact he probably had no need to; they were already terrified. Shankly had insisted that Inter go out first. He kept peering out of the dressing room to see if they had gone. "No, after you," he graciously told them. "Thank you," they replied, and automatically raced down to the Kop end, only to be greeted by a wall of whistles. Such effrontery. But rather than stand their ground they fled towards the other end. It was like the white flag going up. From that moment on they were a defeated side. Minutes later there was an explosion of noise from 54,000 as Gerry Byrne and Gordon Milne appeared from out of the tunnel, the FA Cup held aloft. Anfield erupted. To this day I have still never seen or heard anything like it. Slowly, almost painfully slowly, they paraded around the ground. Then as they approached the Kop, I'll swear the roof was lifted a few inches. Grown men alongside me were in tears, 25,000 of us packed like sardines, swaying one way, then another, all on tip-toes, just to get a glimpse of the Cup.

Within four minutes of the kick off "Sir" Roger Hunt had put Liverpool ahead. But Inter Milan were not world champions for nothing. Five minutes later Mazzola had equalised. Then on the half hour Liverpool were awarded a free kick. Up stepped Callaghan and Stevenson. The little winger ran over the ball, Stevenson looped it into the area and there was Callaghan, unmarked, to poke it into the back of the net. By half time it could have been four but for some mysterious reason the referee disallowed what looked a perfectly good Chris Lawler goal while a goalpost annoyingly got in the way of a Ron Yeats thunderball. But a third goal was inevitable and with just fifteen minutes remaining Callaghan squared the ball to Smith who slipped it to Hunt. The flag stayed down and Ian St John snapped up the rebound from the goalkeeper.

By the time I was out of the ground it was 9.15pm. I had been almost four hours on the Kop, squashed, squeezed and sweating from the overwhelming heat of 25,000 Kopites. I had lost Bill and Pete long since and had ended up at least thirty yards from where I had started but I was happy, deliriously happy. The world champions had been stuffed.

Stephen F. Kelly

3

Liverpool v Ajax
European Cup 1st Round
2nd Leg, 14 December 1966

My most vivid memory of Liverpool in Europe concerns the return leg of the Ajax match on December 14, 1966. After losing the first leg in Holland a week earlier by a 5-1 margin, we were then subjected for the next seven days to the greatest brainwashing that the red half of the City of Liverpool has ever known.

We were being subjected to this by the late, great Bill Shankly! He assured us that the first leg was a freak result, because Ajax wore white shirts and as it was a foggy night our players had not been able to see them coming out of the gloom until it was too late. He told us they were a gang of nobodies; they had never been heard of outside Holland and when we got them on the sacred turf of Anfield we would rip them apart, give them a football lesson and so on. He kept this up for the seven days before the return leg.

Come the day of the match the whole of the Red Army were at fever pitch. All day at work the banter flew around.

"Are you going to the match, Frank?"

"Yeah, we'll batter them, Shanks said!" I'd reply.

7

"Yers have got no chance. They'll probably work three more up yers." This from a Blue Nose working across the line at Fords.

Anyway, home from work, quick bite to eat, washed and dressed (in the swinging sixties smart suit and tie was the norm then!) Then over to the pub to meet my mate Dave Gibson, we had the customary two pints of bitter each and off we go. Loads were waiting at the bus stop in Tunnel Road. Every 26 bus was crampacked with red and white, scarves hanging out of the windows.

"We'll have to walk, Dave" I say. We don't notice the couple of miles go by, as we chat away, how we are going to hammer them. Getting nearer to the ground now, the crowd is thickening and getting noisier. Chanting! singing! laughing! joking! Slowing down now, we come to a dead stop by the Sandon. Bloody hell! this isn't the queue is it? Hang on, it's only a copper up front letting a few cars through. Fifty yards further on it IS the queue. Six or seven people deep to each turnstile, coppers on horses riding in and out. "Hey, get to the back you! That's the front of this queue and that's the back of that one! Pointing to a long snaking line of heaving, pushing, sweating humanity. We moved along slowly, carried mostly by the heaving mass. The atmosphere was electric, with thoughts of things to come. Not far to go now, only ten yards. BANG! What's that? The turnstiles are shutting. The cry goes up "They're shutting the bloody gates!" Blind panic, we run to the next gate, try to squash in the queue. BANG! The sound is repeated all along the entrance to the Kop. Wails and moans go up. Appeals to the gods of three or four different Scouse religions. No reply!

"Come on Dave", I say "let's walk around the ground. We might find a gate open" The two of us, and about five thousand others with the same idea.

We finally get back in front of the Kop, loads of people were still milling around. A copper was riding up and down on the pavement in front of the now defunct turnstiles, in case there was an attempt to go over the top, like something out of World War One.

Dave and I squeeze into the Park pub opposite and manage to get a pint. We stand on stools, gazing out of the window, watching the copper go up and down on his horse, more slowly now there are less people about.

Dave says "I bet one of us can get in. As soon as he's gone past opposite, we'll run over and one of us can clasp hands and bunk the other on top of the wall." The wall was much lower then, but it had old glass stuck on it.

Because I was the smallest and lightest, it was decided I should do the kamikaze stunt. The copper passes. Run! Dave's there first, hands clasped, palms up. I'm coming in fast. Foot in hands, heave! up! up! I nearly cleared the wall, landing on the glass with the thickest part of my coat and a woolly jumper underneath. Out of the corner of my eye I spot Dave sprinting away. I also see the copper, on what now looks like the Grand National winner. Panic! I swing my legs over quickly before he grabs them. Over they go, slipping, my coat rips. Can't grab the wall with the glass! SPLASH! I'm down. I've only gone over where the mens urinals are. I stand up, all in one piece, ankle deep in you know what, (a 53,000 crowd times two pints) drenched down one side. What the hell, I'M IN! I start burrowing my way into my normal spec. "Jeezus, pal, where've you been?" As I worm my way past I hear "He doesn't half pen and ink, him." "Hey, la, why didn't you go to the toilet, ha! ha!" Surprisingly, I am in for the kickoff, and I've plenty of space around me in my old spec, I wonder why?

One minute gone and Peter Thompson crashes a twenty five yard pile driver against the bar! The cry goes up "Come on, Reds - we'll batter these!" But sad to say, we didn't. "Sir" Roger Hunt scored twice, but so did a certain Johan Cruyff, if my memory serves me right. We lost 7-3 overall, but that night we saw the emergence of one of the world's greatest players in Cruyff, and two of the world's best club sides.

And I still went on to believe everything Bill Shankly told me, because I am a LIVERPUDLIAN!

Frank Boyd

4

Liverpool v Borussia Mönchengladbach
UEFA Cup Final
First Leg, 10 May 1973

The game that never was.

Consult any record book (as the ever increasing army of Middle England are increasingly prone to do) and you will find no mention of a biblically proportioned rainstorm which forced the abandonment after twenty eight minutes of the UEFA Cup Final First leg between Liverpool and Borussia Mönchengladbach.

It was too much to expect the elegant skills of German international Gunter Netzer and our very own Tommy Smith to shine on such a pitch. Even the Kopites chant of,

"We want football" (Prehistoric these days maybe, but marginally better than, "You're not singing anymore") and "We're not going home" couldn't persuade the referee to change his mind.

Having negotiated the barbed wire that separated the Boys Pen from the rest of humanity and the free world, better known as the Spion Kop, it was a wee bit annoying to find that the break "over the top" had all been in vain. All the Pen escapees headed for the wall at the back of the Kop, simply because it was the nearest and only place we could see from. This vantage point didn't afford the luxury of a view of the centre circle or the Anfield Road goal. We glimpsed the Kop Goal, a few yards more, then nothing, apart from the thousands of Kopites heads, squirming around quizzically, peering up at us. It made us feel good, staring down at all those men who had paid to get in. When the goalkeeper disappeared from view, the news filtered through to us that the game had been postponed. Postponement meant money for the replay and ensured that the interminable battle with the authorities and the elements for illegal access to the hallowed shrine of the Kop would begin again. For ninety per cent of the Boys Pen detainees there was only one thought on admission - to get out. Sandwiched between an indifferent Main Stand and the populous and empathetic Kopites, the Pen was a heaving cauldron of Liverpool's underclass. You watched your pockets and, as tradition dictated, spat through the wire mesh at people in the obstructed view seats in the Main Stand. Fraternity and the Pen most certainly didn't go hand in hand.

A hastily cobbled together meeting of UEFA officials resulted in the seemingly bizarre decision to replay the game the very next night. Liverpool, with uncharacteristic altruism, decided on a flat charge of ten pence entrance for the game. The gates opened at 5.30 to cope with the expected rush, which strangely enough never materialised. The gate that night was 41,000, some 4,000 less than the previous night's washout.

I seized the opportunity and ventured into the Paddock, for the simple reason that I had never been in there before.

The Paddock was a curious mix of men in camel coats and women wearing home made knitted scarves passing flasks of tea around at half-time. This was light years away from the uncovered refreshment bar in the Boys Pen, which stood not a million miles away from a gents toilet in the Kop. The escape route onto the Kop via this toilet trod a particularly dangerous path. It required mountaineering expertise as you had to drop down, literally, into the toilet. On the night of the postponed game I had witnessed a sickening fall. The pungent smell and the protests from the relieving Kopites was usually enough of a deterrent; the majority dropping back again down onto the Pen steps, preferring to tackle the barbed wire again.

A Shankly tactical switch meant "Little Bamber" Brian Hall being replaced with a brooding John Toshack, who hadn't played for two months. Brian has suffered the same fate as many Liverpool players down the years, i.e. a dodgy media-invented nickname, credited to witty Kopites. Anyway, Toshack for Hall worked. The Reds won 3-0 thanks largely to a classic aerial display from our ex-Cardiff man, but the Clemence penalty save (one of the best I've ever seen) gets scant recognition.

The Reds took a three goal advantage to Borussia and uncannily survived a pre-match storm. They conceded two goals in twenty minutes, but became the first English club to win the League Championship and a European trophy in the same season.

Mick Potter

5

Glory Years

As we all know, football supporters have a tendency towards wild exaggeration, sweeping generalisations and a sentimental nostalgia for the good old days. It seems that the golden age is never the present age. Dewy-eyed yearning for long gone days can easily give way to false memory syndrome, but this is patently the romance of football and the beauty of the game. Opinions masquerade as facts. Events, goals, careers, seasons and cup upsets all blur into fiction. We shelter in folklore, legend and the safety and certainty of the past. After all, it is there in black and white, documented in a plethora of publications, but the good thing about history is that it is adaptable and subjective. The authorised versions of Liverpool F.C. do not reflect what it was really like to be in those magnificent cities during that period.

It is no wonder that supporters of Liverpool F.C. have good memories and fertile imaginations. It is almost impossible to conjure up too much excitement for an F.A. Cup fixture at Gay Meadow, Shrewsbury on a Sunday morning when your team has lifted the European Cup in Paris and Rome. No matter how many "Fantasy Football" type bores or F.A. Cup romantics witter on about David and Goliath giant killing acts, to Liverpudlians a Tuesday

night replay at Hartlepool is always going to be more inspiring than a week in the Eternal City, isn't it?

Paris and Rome, the mere mention of these cities reduces Liverpool fans to uncontrollable fits of emotion. They are etched in the collective psyche of Liverpool supporters, the venues of three of Liverpool's four European Cup victories. As with all great clubs with a haughty sense of superiority, glamour means only one thing, to be Champions of Europe. Recent forays into Europe may have wetted the insatiable appetite of Liverpudlians, but they also have a depressing familiarity to them. Unpredictable performances leading to early exits from the Cup Winners Cup and the UEFA Cup. These failures have inevitably induced a restless pining for the great nights in Europe. Everything else recedes into insignificance. All glory may well be fleeting, but Liverpool's lasted longer than most, from the UEFA Cup victory in 1973 to the tragic night in Brussels.

Nurtured on the culture of success, Liverpool fans dream of trips to the San Siro or the Bernabeu, not tickets to the new "Findus Stand" in Grimsby. This may seem cruel and condescending, and of course it is. It also happens to be the truth. Penne alla Vongole near the Trevi Fountain or cod and chips in a Grimsby chippy. I rest my case, your honour. "Allez les Rouges" and bring on the Europeans or let me revel in my memories.

Peter Hooton

14

6

Liverpool v Borussia Mönchengladbach
European Cup Final
Rome, 25th May 1977

At the time it seemed a brilliant idea. Travel to Italy to see Liverpool in the European Cup Final. The one slight drawback was that it would mean travelling by train, the plus points were that it was the cheapest deal on offer, and, like the chartered flights, it also included a match ticket. How could we refuse? Wembley and the disappointment of the previous weekend was already forgotten, we never really had time to dwell on the fact that we'd lost out on the chance of being the first ever team to win the treble (League, FA Cup and European Cup). It was practically a case of just arrive home on Sunday and prepare for the journey to Folkestone on the Monday.

Demand, as you might expect, was enormous. Trains from all over the country were brought in to cope with the extremely high number of bookings. After arriving in Ostend very early, we discovered that we had to take the "scenic route", which meant covering half of Europe. Once we arrived in Rome, we found a bus that would take us to the stadium and went to have our first look. We were very

impressed by the sight that greeted us, which wasn't difficult when you've only ever had Wembley to compare it with! Then it was a case of freshen up and wander about the town all day.

The longer the day went, the more Liverpool supporters we met. It seemed as if Liverpool had been transferred to Italy for the day! Almost before we realised, it was time to make our way to the Olympic Stadium. We got there about an hour before kick off and we couldn't believe the number of people decked out in red and white. With this kind of support, we couldn't possibly lose. We outnumbered Borussia Mönchengladbach by something like three to one!

The teams took to the pitch and kicked off. Liverpool got off to a dream start after twenty minutes when Terry McDermott ran on to a through ball and placed it in the corner of the net. 1-0 Liverpool. Liverpool started to take control of the game but didn't make too many more chances, still 1-0 wasn't bad. At least we weren't losing.

As the game went on, Borussia started to come more and more into it, and it was no surprise when Alan Simonsen, Borussia's Danish international striker, took the ball midway into Liverpool's half and hit an unstoppable shot past Ray Clemence. 1-1. This seemed to rock Liverpool and for a while they looked as if they were going to be totally outplayed. Half time and the scores were still level.

The second half started the way the first had ended, Borussia having more of the chances, while Liverpool were looking increasingly unsteady. Borussia hit the post and continued to attack. I thought, "Oh my god, we're gonna get battered here". Ray Clemence made a brilliant save from yet another Borussia attack, and then it was as if the team had suddenly realised that they were here to make a game of it. After soaking up what seemed like unbearable pressure, Liverpool started to come back into the game, applying some of their own. Eventually they managed to break out of their own half! It was from one of these attacks that the turning point came. Liverpool forced a corner and sent almost everyone up. Steve Heighway took the kick and almost from nowhere Tommy Smith appeared and headed the ball into the back of the net. More wild celebrations from the exported City of Liverpool and this time the unspoken conviction that this was it. One thing about Liverpool in those days, they rarely made the same mistake twice, and so it proved on this occasion. Midfield and defence combined to tighten the game up and supply the forward line with more chances.

Kevin Keegan, playing his last game for Liverpool, played his last ace. All through the night he gave Berti Vogts the run around and left him chasing shadows. On this last occasion he was running towards the goal when he was tripped by Vogts. Penalty!

Phil Neal was coolness personified. He very rarely missed from the spot, but then he'd never taken a penalty as important as this. If he missed it might just give the Germans enough of a chance to draw level again. If he scored though, it was all over. He placed the ball calmly on the spot, walked back, and waited for the referee to give him the signal. The tension was almost unbearable. I was half tempted to cover my eyes, then I thought, if I do that and he scores I'll have missed it. The ref blew, Neal ran up. The goalie dived to his left, Neal hit the ball to his right into the back of the net. "IT'S THERE! THAT'S IT! 3-1!"

Totally in control now, Liverpool just had to take it nice and easy and wait for the final whistle. The ninety minutes were up, but the ref showed no sign of blowing for the end yet. Ninety two minutes, "Come on ref! How much injury time are you playing?" Ninety three minutes... the final whistle. "YES! WE'VE DONE IT! "WE ARE THE CHAMPIONS, CHAMPIONS OF EUROPE" Emlyn Hughes goes up in front of the stands and receives the trophy. "RAAYYY," "NICE ONE, EMLYN, NICE ONE SON, NICE ONE EMLYN, LET'S HAVE ANOTHER ONE". All the players come over to where the City of Liverpool was standing cheering on the terraces and acknowledge the fans. That season, the link between the

team and supporters seemed to be summed up by one player more than the others and that was Joey Jones. With everyone singing his name, he could hardly wait to get his medal and come over to greet "his mates". As you might expect of Joey, he was never one for half measures! He came running across the park draped in a union flag and wearing a home made top hat given to him by one of the fans. The scoreboards were totally blank except for one word in the centre.

* * * * * * * * * * * * * *

LIVERPOOL

* * * * * * * * * * * * * *

The journey back to Liverpool seemed even longer than the journey out, and, as a result we missed Tommy Smith's testimonial match back in England. Nobody cared though.

Barry Stone

18

7

Fiat to the Rescue

After the great night at Anfield when Liverpool defeated St.Etienne, my brother, Tucker, and I decided to do all we could to go to Rome on 25 May for the European Cup Final assuming we beat Zurich in the semi-final! That proved to be no problem and after some begging, some borrowing and cashing in a life insurance policy we raised the money to go to Rome.

The morning of Wednesday May 25th soon came and at 6.00 a.m. we were at Speke Airport boarding a Freddy Laker "Skytrain". By the time we arrived at Leonardo da Vinci airport we had drunk the plane dry! We were met at the airport by a coach that took us to the Colosseum after a quick tour of the city.

The afternoon was free, so we went to find the Spanish Steps and the Trevi Fountain and, of course, a few bars.I think the wine was about 90p a gallon! But that didn't matter as we had about one million lire and lots of sweets and matches given as change. By now we had met up with a couple of other lads and also spoken to a few Germans who were amazed at some of the flags and banners and also at how many "Reds" there were in Rome.

The afternoon had been magic and we still had the match itself to come.

At 5 o'clock we were back at the Colosseum which was now decked out in red and white. By 6 o'clock we realised that our coach wasn't going to turn up and we had better make our own way to the ground. Just then a little Fiat 500 stopped. " Any chance of a lift to the Olympic Stadium?" I asked the Italian driver. Quick as a flash, four of us jumped in the car only to find a headstone on the back seat. The Italian was obviously a mason or perhaps a gravedigger. "It will be alright, just get in", said the driver, "I will take you there for some lire". "Right lads, empty your pockets, this fellow wants money," I said. I started counting out the notes onto the dashboard and soon there was enough to satisfy the Italian. Eventually we were in sight of the ground we'd made it! Along with 25,000 other supporters.

The match, the night, the team, the fans all were fantastic. We won 3-1 with goals from McDermott, Smith and Neal. Now all we had to do was get back to the airport by midnight for the return flight. We managed that with no problems and arrived home at 6 o'clock on Thursday morning. We went to work in a daze, but we weren't dreaming. Liverpool had won the European Cup for the first time.

Alan Adlington

8

Dancing in the Trevi Fountain

In 1977 Liverpool reached the final of the European Cup for the first time. I was sixteen and it was exam time but I was determined to get to Rome come what may. I cancelled my exams and signed up for another year at 6th Form College to do my "O" Levels. The problem was how to get there, and more importantly, how to persuade my Dad to pay for me!

Walking home from school one Friday night I saw the answer to my prayers in Pickford Travel's window:

Rimini, Italy,

7 Days in May for £46

I rushed straight home to tell my Dad and to my surprise he said, "Yes".

On Saturday morning two of us went down to Pickfords to book. The girl behind the counter said, "You are the 19th and 20th people to book that trip today, what's going on in Italy?" When we told her she couldn't believe it.

So we had a week in a hotel on the beach with a swimming pool and, for £17, Cosmos laid on a coach to take us to Rome for the final and back to Rimini the following day. Me and my mates had a great time by the sea, rounded off by a terrific win by Liverpool in Rome. In fact the only bad part was getting a talking to off my Dad for dancing in the Trevi Fountain after the match!

Paul Burton

9

Letting the Train take the Strain

Imagine the scene: a coach full of happy but badly drunken Liverpool supporters travelling back from the 1977 Rome victory over Borussia Mönchengladbach. In the small hours, our coach reached the Brenner Pass in the Alps between Italy and Austria. Although it was May, the road was snowbound and impassable, so unknown to the coachload of sleeping drunks, the driver decided to take the coach through the Brenner Pass railway tunnel on the rail transporter.

Picture the mass confusion as all the drunks gradually awoke in total darkness, sitting on a coach, but hearing the sound of train wheels on a railway line! The last thing I remember before slipping back into a drunken stupour was somebody saying, "That vino must be good stuff. I thought we were on a coach, but we must have caught the train instead!"

Rob Connor

10

Borussia Mönchengladbach v Liverpool
European Cup Semi-Final
1st leg, 29th March 1978

After all the *fun* we'd encountered on our last journey across Europe by train (i.e. the "infamous trip to Rome") you'd have to have parts missing to consider doing the same thing again, yet, not 12 months after that, here we were setting off for yet another trans-European adventure! About a week before the semi-final of the 1978 European Cup Liverpool were playing a league match at home. That morning I got a phone call from one of my mates who was interested in going to Germany. "British Rail are running trains to the semi's; it's only £36 and that includes yer match ticket". Not too surprisingly, I did have doubts in the back of my mind but, I thought, "they'll have learned their lesson from last year, and anyway, Germany's nowhere near as far as Rome"!

We got to Lime Street Station, and this time we were better prepared for the long journey down to Folkestone; we'd bought the equivalent of a rain forest to read on the way and settled for another interesting journey. As we'd figured, this time there wasn't the same demand as there

had been for the final in Rome the year before, but there was enough interest to fill two trains. Early the following morning, we arrived in Ostend and boarded the train. As usual, wherever the Kop travel away they like to announce themselves in grand style, and this trip was no different. Everyone was decked out in red and white, and we all carried flags and banners of some description. As soon as everyone was on, the train left the station and we all settled back.

The one thing you realise about travelling to football matches, especially by train, is that football *specials* are anything but that! Nobody cared though, because we hardly spent any of the journey sitting down, most of the time we just stood in the passageway, watching the scenery pass us by and hung out of the windows cheering and waving our banners and flags whenever we went through a station. Eventually, we reached our destination, now the main worry was how far away from the station was the ground and how did we get there? The answers to both these questions were provided as soon as we walked outside and saw that any trams that were going to the Rheinstadium had a small green square board on the front with a drawing of a football on it. When we arrived we had another opportunity to see just how poorly served English football fans are by having just one, years old national stadium, which is supposed to be the centrepiece of our national sport! The game kicked off, and Liverpool went in to their well organised routine for European away ties - defend and hit Borussia on the break. This worked well and we went in at half time 0-0.

In the second half, Borussia started to apply a little more pressure and forced Liverpool back a bit further, and it was no surprise when they scored. Watching all the celebrating we thought to ourselves "if it stays like this it won't be too bad, we'll beat then in the second leg at Anfield", but even better was to come. Borussia now started to press home their advantage and for a short while it became a matter of Liverpool hanging on to make sure that they didn't concede another goal. Suddenly, Liverpool broke, and Ray Kennedy passed a through ball to David Johnson

• Reykjavik to Rome • Reykjavik to Rome • Reykjavik to Rome • Reykjavik to Rome •

who hit the ball low into the corner of the net. This was even better than being 1-0 down, because now we had the away goal and we also had Borussia where we wanted them.

Liverpool fans en route for Mönchengladbach

The joy didn't last too long though. We hardly stopped celebrating our goal when the referee awarded a free kick against Liverpool, about 20 yards from the Liverpool area. Rainer Bonhoff, one of many internationals playing on both sides that night, stepped up and hit a piledriver of a shot that seemed to turn all different ways in the air before hitting the back of the net. The goal barely had time to sink in before the referee blew his whistle for full-time. All the way back to the station we were all talking about the game that we'd just seen, and were still convinced that we weren't in any danger of losing. "We got the away goal and we'll make that count at Anfield".

All that night travelling back through Germany, whenever we stopped at a station, either to pick up mail for delivery or morning papers to be sent further down the line, railway staff took great delight in telling us the score from earlier.

"Yeah, but don't forget that we scored, and that means that we've got an away goal", we said.

They all just thought that we were trying to put a brave face on things and shook their heads and laughed!

Barry Stone

11

Setting out for Wembley

Liverpool v FC Bruges
European Cup Final
London, 10th May 1978

My son Kevin, who was seven years old at the time, asked if there was any chance of me taking him to the 1978 European Cup Final at Wembley. I told him I'd see what I could do. Luckily, I managed to get tickets for the game and then booked seats on the train.

A few days before the match, I came home from work one night and said to Kevin, "Do you want to go to this game with me, then?" and gave him the envelope. When he opened it and saw the tickets inside, he was "made up" to say the least! It was worth it for my wife, Jean, and myself just to see to see his face light up with excitement.

We went down to London on the train, had two smashing meals, and, when Liverpool won the cup it made a very special day even better. When we arrived home Kevin said "The day and the atmosphere at the match was just electric." The whole experience, especially as it was Kevin's first European Cup Final, is one we will all treasure for many years to come.

Billy Flanagan

12

Little Davie

Every time I watch the European Cup Final and see some soccer giant from Marseille or AC Milan hoisting the European Cup aloft I can't help but think of Little Davie. Platini, Cruyff, Beckenbauer, Gullit, Dalglish, Puskas. All the famous names of European football have at some time lifted that great trophy above their heads. If only they knew what I know. But then they don't know anything about Little Davie and the European Cup .

Little Davie used to work for a television company, not a million miles from Liverpool. And as his name suggests he was only small, no more than 5ft 3ins but packed into his spindly frame was a laugh-a-minute. Well, some years ago about September, when Liverpool set about defending their European Cup, the local TV sports programme decided it would be a good idea if they had the European Cup in the studio. "It could sit on the desk alongside the presenter," suggested Young Davie, "and they could fix the camera on it as they began to talk about Liverpool's tricky defence of the trophy." The producer agreed that it would look good shining in the studio lights. All they had to do was ask Liverpool if they could borrow it.

Little Davie was assigned the delicate task of phoning the club. "No problem," said a generous Peter Robinson. "Anytime. Just send a taxi to pick it up."

"But what shall we do about getting it back ?" asked Davie. "Will you still be there later tonight."

"Oh dear, no." replied Peter Robinson. "I tell you what," he added, "why don't you hang on to it overnight and send it back in the morning. Have you got somewhere safe for it ?"

"Oh aye," replied the producer, grabbing the phone to reassure Peter Robinson, "we can lock it away in the company safe." All was agreed and a couple of hours before the show began the trophy duly arrived in its large leather bound case in a taxi.

In the studio the Cup was carefully positioned, pride of place, next to the presenter, Gerald Sinstadt. Only the floor manager was allowed to touch it while admiring technicians hovered enviously. All went well with the show. Various players past and present assessed Liverpool's chances of winning it again and there was plenty of footage of previous Liverpool triumphs. Afterwards Davie was congratulating himself telling everyone he had thought of the idea first . "Let's adjourn to the bar," suggested the now relaxed producer. "I'll just put this in the safe upstairs first," he said picking up the Cup. So off went the producer in search of the company safe somewhere on the sixth floor. As arranged, the security guard was on hand. The safe was carefully unlocked. But then they discovered a problem nobody had thought of. The Cup wouldn't fit. As everyone knows, the European Cup is at least three and a half feet high and when in it's box its another foot bigger all around.

"Oh hell," said the producer, or words to that effect. But even with all his cursing there was no way it was going to fit. "Have we got another safe ?" he asked.

"No," replied a weary security guard who wondered why these football experts hadn't thought of this dilemma before.

"We've got a problem," the producer told the lads back in the office. "It won't fit so someone is going to have look after it overnight. I'm going away for the weekend so I can hardly take it with me or leave it on the back seat of the car. - Davie," he roared, "you'll have to take care of it."

A startled Davie looked up. "Oh ay, boss, why me ?"

"Because one of these other buggers 'll lose it," he replied sharply, "and anyhow you were claiming it was your idea, so you should have thought about this problem in the first place. Just look after it tonight and send it back to Anfield tomorrow. Come on, let's go to the pub."

So Little Davie picked up the mighty trophy, the most coveted possession in European soccer and clutching his briefcase made his way to the bar with the others, his head barely visible over the top of the large leather box. He fumbled his way down the stairs and across the road to the pub.

"What you got there Davie?" asked some of his pals.

"The European Cup," he sniggered, "Honestly..." The Cup was duly placed in a corner and the serious business of drinking commenced.

"Mind you don't lose it," joked the producer an hour later as he got up to leave, "or you'll find yourself on the front page of every newspaper in Europe!" Numerous pints later and with all the sports department now long gone, Davie decided it was time for home. He phoned a taxi, picked up his bag and wandered outside to wait for the cab. Minus, of course, the European Cup. But just as Davie flopped into the seat of the taxi, someone dashed out of the pub. "Davie is that your box in the corner?"

"Christ!" screamed Davie, dashing back into the pub and removing the various pint pots that were perched on top of the case. "Thanks," he called to the barman as he staggered back out with his prize possession, the cold sweat still showing on his forehead.

Outside Davie's home he hauled the box out of the back seat of the cab and staggered up the path where he rang the doorbell. A startled son answered the door.

"What you got there Dad ?" he asked.

"What's it look like. The European Cup of course," snapped Davie visibly tiring of the same question.

"Get away Dad," replied a don't-try-and-kid-me smart-arsed son.

"No, honestly, it's the European Cup. I've got to look after it."

Now Davie's lad was of an impressionable age, all of ten, a football fanatic. You know the sort. His eyes shot out like stalks as Dad unlocked the case and pulled the glittering trophy out.

"Here," he said, "clear that vase and the photo of Grandma off the sideboard and let's put it up there." And so the European Cup was placed neatly on top of Little Davie's telly for the evening and the two of them sat back to admire it. Even Davie's wife was impressed.

Davie had his tea and had hardly noticed that his son was missing when there was a banging at the door. He went to open it and found standing in front of him, or rather should I say, stretching down the path and into the road, a queue of his son's pals and their fathers. All were clutching cameras.

"Some of my mates want to have their photos taken with the cup," announced Davie Junior. Aye, more likely it's their Dads who want to be photographed, thought Davie.

"Come on then. One at a time." he agreed. And so, one by one Davie Junior's pals were invited into the sitting room to glare at the trophy, pick it up and have their photos taken. The procedure went on all night. Everyone in the street wanted a go. The news spread quickly. Even old Mrs Grimshaw came tottering down the road for a snap. All

that remains to be said is that somewhere in the north of England there is a terraced street where all the youngsters have a precious photograph of themselves standing in Little Davie's front room clutching the European Cup. Just like all those famous names. The following morning the heavy old trophy was returned to Anfield, its secret assured. That is until now as I've just blown the gaff. And so the next time you see some international soccer star lifting that famous old trophy high above his head or see a photograph of it resplendent in the Anfield boardroom, think of Little Davie and the kids in his street and the night the European Cup sat on their sideboard.

Stephen F. Kelly.

13

Oulu Palloseura v Liverpool
European Cup
1st Round, 1st leg 17th September 1980

In September 1980 my friend Peter O'Brien from Rock Ferry and I decided that wherever Liverpool played in Europe that season we would go. Well, the draw was made and we got Oulu of Finland! After a lot of searching on the map to find the place, we were off to the Transalpino ticket office near the University. The cost was £114.10 and I've still got the ticket.

The journey started on Saturday night after a home game, travelling from Lime Street to London. On Sunday morning our journey took us to Harwich, the Hook of Holland and Hamburg, eventually arriving in Copenhagen on Monday. From Copenhagen we travelled by train and boat to Stockholm; then by boat to Turku where we arrived at 8.00 a.m. on Tuesday morning. We finally arrived at Oulu, a small town on the edge of the Arctic Circle, at 6.00 p.m. on Tuesday, after a non-stop journey of 66 hours!

After arriving in Oulu we met all the players in their hotel. The match was played the following day and we were due to start back at midnight the same day. If we caught that train and made all our connections we could make the

Reykjavik to Rome • Reykjavik to Rome • Reykjavik to Rome • Reykjavik to Rome • Reykjavik to Rome •

away match at Southampton on the Saturday. We had no tickets for the match but when Phil Neal heard about our problem he promised us six tickets at Southampton if we made it in time. Sure enough, we did and there were the tickets.

On the journey home my best friend, Peter, met a girl on the boat from Turku to Stockholm. After exchanging letters Peter and Paula eventually married in Rovanimi, Paula's home town in Finland. Peter now lives in Helsinki but still has a season ticket for Anfield and comes home quite often to see the "Reds" and travels to all the European away matches.

Paul Burton

14

Liverpool v Real Madrid
European Cup Final
Paris, 27th May 1981

I haven't been to many European games with Liverpool, because I am terrified of flying. The best though was the European Cup Final in Paris against Real Madrid. For a start, I got to carry Bill Shankly's bags from his hotel to the coach taking him back to the airport.

Every one says the final was boring, but seeing Alan Kennedy's goal go in was one of the great moments of my life - like the days our children were born - and any match in which your team wins the European Cup isn't going to be too boring, is it?

Afterwards we took over a bar in the centre of Paris. We had been told that the Parisians were unfriendly and resented us, but our Parisians were great. They joined in our singing and even in the beer fight we had later in the evening. We were turned out in the small hours. We, French and English alike, stood outside in the street and sang the most beautiful version of "You'll Never Walk Alone" there ever was.

Not much of a story, I suppose, but I have seldom been happier.

John Peel

15

Paris Match

Paris, rich in historical symbolism, the birthplace of revolutionary fervour, the centre of fashion and gastronomic delights, was playing host to the European Cup Final. The mere mention of the place induced a sort of fevered anticipation. We were leaving Liverpool to sample the excesses of Paris. For the weeks leading up to the departure we must have been unbearable. We were smug, boastful and our conversation was two dimensional, how to get there and what we were going to do when we arrived.

We were young, free and single, convinced of our immortality and the certainty of meaningless yet pleasurable

36

relationships with the suave, impressionable maidens of Paris. We arrived at St Lazare station in the centre of Paris on the Sunday before the match. We may well have been the least sexy creatures ever to arrive in Paris after an overnight journey from Liverpool, but nothing a bath and a clean pair of underpants wouldn't fix. The journey had been relatively uneventful apart from the duty free contents being redistributed to the needy, which warranted a water canon hosedown by the thoughtful gendarmes at Dieppe. The felons, as is usually the case, disembarked bone-dry, but for the rest of us, five hundred or so souls, it was a sobering wake up call as we crossed the gangplank, drenched from head to foot.

Nevertheless, it was a blessing in disguise as we were able to enjoy the beautiful French countryside wide-eyed on the train to Paris, and, of course, practise our imaginative chat-up lines for Parisian barmaids "Une pinte de bière et un packet de durex s'il vous plâit"

St Lazare resembled Victoria Station architecturally and was just as busy on the day we arrived. Our intrepid group of travellers alighted from the train glowing with expectation. We swaggered with self confidence, only to be greeted with blank incomprehension from urbane Parisians. A small group of fellow Liverpudlians were at the station to greet us, but by and large we were the first group to arrive en masse, courtesy of a Transalpino scam. Left out of the station, up the hill a bit and voilà, we found our ideal hotel. Cheap and cheerful with no attention to detail. Suffice it to say it wasn't listed in the Michelin guide, but it had a certain "Fawlty" type charm. It was less than five minutes away from the station, but more importantly away from the madhouse right next door to the station which had been commandeered by a rather large group of volatile, flagwaving xenophobes destined for the Bastille.

We settled in and after a touch of personal grooming we were off to be corrupted by models. We found ourselves inexplicably drawn to the Pigalle, like priests to Lourdes. Heads turned when we entered bars and we convinced ourselves that everyone thought we were fascinating. The

Pigalle, the notorious red light area didn't disappoint and it became a magnet for many a hapless Scouser fascinated by the forbidden fruits of the expensive bordello. Stripjoints, arcades, sex shops, brothels, jazz clubs, and colourful restaurants teeming with nocturnal creatures, the place had it all. It also had a strange and worrying fascination for our group of ten fresh faced youngsters from Liverpool who had only just broken the shackles of Catholic school indoctrination.

Society and living at home with your mum may well teach us certain restraints of acceptable behaviour, but we were determined to shelve our repressed emotions and indulge in an orgy of hedonism and debauchery. Even though the Pigalle had a reputation we knew we were safe, not only in numbers, but received wisdom had it that pimps wouldn't tolerate mean streets as they are bad for business. So we headed for a brightly lit plaza quite near the Moulin Rouge and set up camp in a very busy bar being served enormous glasses of beer. Over the next few nights our bar became a meeting point and we built up a rapport with the locals. As the beer flowed we abandoned misplaced hopes of charming young females back to our hotel and loosened our vocal chords in preparation for the big match. It was the street walkers time to look astonished as their hang out resounded to the guttural strains of "on the dole, in Paree, drinking wine."

Meanwhile, back at St Lazare and the Hotel from Hell, our intuition had been proved correct and a very shady street adjacent to the station (aren't they all?) had been cordoned of by the enthusiastic riot police. This street was frequented by gentlemen who preferred prostitutes of the more mature variety. These grannies stood in doorways clutching dying flowers, but the irony was lost on them. Presumably the punters, pre - AIDS, were fascinated by the horrendous skin complaints most of them proudly showed off on their weary legs. It appeared that trouble erupted after guffaws and catcalls from the boisterous "let's stay near the station" mob of Liverpudlians. The pimps had not taken too kindly to the merriment, and were worried that their clients would be put off, so they decided to "clean up" their territory which resulted in the inevitable communication breakdown and a night of incarceration for many of the insurgents.

The following day we abandoned plans to visit places of interest like Notre Dame, the Louvre or even the Eiffel Tower, because we were off in search of fashion and heading to the Boulevard St Germain in a desperate search for the mythical Adidas Centre which was rumoured to stock training shoes unavailable in Blighty. It wasn't that we were philistines, it's just that you have to cater for the whole group on excursions like this, and several of our group thought we would be "cooler" and "sexier" if they were able to locate what we now know to be the nonexistent trainer: the Adidas Holy Grail. Culture was abandoned and the race was on. After a spectacularly unsuccessful day asking incredulous Parisians, "Où est le centre d' Adidas?" our hopeless group unconvincingly agreed that the day had been well spent. The indigenous population were probably not impressed with being asked for a fictional shop by cocky youths with wedge haircuts when there was so much to see in their magnificent city. We continued the search until the day of the match. Some of the uninitiated may see this as a criminal waste of time, but to us it made sense; it gave us our "raison d'être" and also enabled us to see innumerable monuments and buildings - if only fleetingly.

Each afternoon our band of merry men would discuss at length the possibility of a cultural evening, but inevitably we would find ourselves back in the Pigalle. We had all convinced ourselves that we would fall in love with an Algerian belly dancer and rescue her from a life of sin and depravity. After all, we were spectacularly at ease with members of the opposite sex so long as they couldn't understand what we were saying and therefore expose us as shallow vacuous bores who were totally inexperienced.

Whatever it was, we were blissfully happy in our chosen haunt and that was the way it was going to stay.

To the clients who indulged in the pleasures of a meaningless encounter we must have seemed pathetic creatures, cheering every time a "fille de joie" disappeared into a block of flats with one of their number. It seems puerile now, but what a fine time we had, and how we laughed. You will be reassured that our guilt complex prevented any of our party indulging in the sins of the flesh. We were useless, drowning our sorrows in copious amounts of alcohol which left us revoltingly drunk but content. There was a glimmer of hope when one of our party convinced himself that the peep show artist had given him "the eye" and invited him downstairs for a drink. He came back certain that he had found his first true love. We

didn't want to shatter his dreams. It was a cruel world and he had to find out the hard way. After a bit of moral encouragement he went back in, adamant that she fancied him because of his John Lennon mop top, circa 1965. He was relieved of his money and his pride by two staggeringly humourless sumo wrestlers who charged him a weeks wages for two glasses of coke. Conversation and extras were out of his price range so he couldn't even try out his chat up line that he thought would clinch the romance, namely "I come from a long line of Celtic warriors." Oh, how we laughed, laughed with nervous relief that the humiliation had not been ours.

Our hopes of romance fading fast we turned our attention to exhausting the back catalogues of the Jam, the Clash and the Beatles. We knew the words to many a classic song and we held the attention of the whole plaza and all of a sudden we were popular, but mainly with fat balding men from Merseyside.

We never did find the Adidas Centre, but we did return a few months later to see all the historic places of interest. The women with the flowers were still there, in a less volatile environment.

Oh yes, the match! Well Alan Kennedy scored and we beat the mighty Real Madrid one nil, in a pretty uneventful game. And where did we celebrate this famous victory into the wee small hours? You've guessed it, the Pigalle. We were flushed with success and shimmering with self importance, but we still never had any success with the opposite sex. C'est la vie.

Peter Hooton

16

Karrang!

I travelled by coach and ferry to this game with the original Liverpool Supporters' Club which is based in Lower Breck Road, not far from Liverpool's Anfield stadium. This was a very exciting time for me because it was the first European Cup Final involving Liverpool that I had been able to get a ticket for. To see the "Mighty Reds" against the Spanish league champions in Paris would be a dream come true, especially if we won!

This particular time was special for another reason. I have always been a fan of Heavy Metal music and the first ever colour magazine called "Karrang!" was issued just in time for the trip. I was able to read it over and over on the coach and help pass the time.

One memory of France is of seeing armed police everywhere, looking very nervous, but, when they started meeting Liverpool fans who were trying to be friendly, giving the police scarves and having their photographs taken with them, then the tension around the Parc Des Princes stadium relaxed and there were smiles everywhere.

The best memory, of course, is of being at the end of the stadium where Alan Kennedy scored the goal that won the match for Liverpool. Winning 1-0 made it a very special day. A Frenchman in the crowd asked me for my scarf for his son, who was with him. They followed St.Etienne, the marvellous French team that Liverpool had played two fabulous games against in the European Cup triumph of 1977, so how could I refuse?

Stuart G. Provost

17

Pre-season friendlies
Man Overboard (Allegedly)

In the early '80s, football was only half the reason we used to go abroad to see Liverpool. A pretty small half, at that. Spotty, unattractive teenagers like ourselves always believed that by crossing La Manche we'd be transformed into charming, irresistible Eurostuds. It was a well-known fact that *all* foreign girls found Liverpudlians fascinating, even though no-one in Merseyside would give us the time of day, so trips to exotic outposts like Athens and Munich were eagerly anticipated. Nobody actually *met* any girls, but in our fevered minds we knew that they were out there.

So it was that one balmy July morning in 1982 we boarded Crown Executive Euroline Plus Coach 2 at Crown Coaches old HQ in Rockford Lane. It was the last word in penury. Hard seats, no toilets, obviously no video or microwave in those days and, as a thoughtful little touch, the exhaust fumes seeped in through a loose flap in the flooring. After a pick-up in Wavertree we were off. Off on a three-day cultural excursion to Bruges for a pre-season tournament that included FC Bruges themselves, Lockeren and the then unknown Sampdoria. Everyone was calling them Sampadoria, which seemed to sound better.

As part of the ritual of going abroad, it was customary to imbibe enormous quantities of liquor at every available waking moment. Crown Coaches had cunningly tried to ban any booze from the trip. A futile measure. Although no actual cans of Tartan or Colt 45 made it on to the coach, dozens of flasks were produced along with curiously scented cigarettes which kept us all happy until Dover.

We boarded a night ferry to Ostend. The sight of the Duty Free shop transformed the company from models of restraint into howling, slobbering cave-dwellers. A few of us who had been going to away games together for a couple of seasons, purchased the raw materials needed for our now customary night cap, The Roger Moore. These were basically very strong Vodka Martinis, without the olive and the little cocktail stick. We used Silver Label Smirnoff, the best available on P&O, and mixed it with Noilly Prat Vermouth and, criminally, lemonade. It was drunk enthusiastically from pint glasses, which were regularly recharged. We were crawling around on all fours before the chalky cliffs of Albion were out of sight.

Much singing and merriment ensued. It is at this point that I must make readers aware of a small but essential item of sub-plot. In the few years leading up to 1982, our family had been hit by one tragedy after another, the most recent being the death of my brother. Since his death, my mother had been very reticent about me going anywhere beyond the kitchen and trips abroad were a particular source of anxiety to her. No matter to me. I was young, selfish and absolutely determined, since the deaths, to have the best possible time out of every day available.

So it was no surprise to those who knew me when, after our conga had wound its way onto the top deck of the ferry, I decided to lower the Union Jack and raise a splendid, if tatty Liver Bird in its place. I made fairly steady progress up the mast-cum-flagpole, when, disastrously, I decided to look down and wave to the chaps. That was the last they saw of me for a little while. I lost my balance and fell spectacularly at least fifteen feet into one of the many

lifeboats which adorned the top deck and the sides of the ferry. A very cosy little lifeboat. So cosy, in fact, that I snuggled up under some heavy tarpaulin-type stuff and set about sleeping off my Roger Moores.

I woke up with teeth chattering and stiff limbs, but otherwise feeling fine. I went off to find the rest of the mob. We were actually coming into dock. Perfect, although I would've liked a breakfast. Never mind. In a couple of hours we'd be sitting at a Bruges pavement cafe enjoying the sunshine with a couple of beers and a sandwich. Life was good. I made my way down to the coach deck to join up with the party. I couldn't immediately see our plush charabanc so, just to make sure they didn't go without me, I went out to the ramp and counted the coaches off the ferry. I wasn't worried when ten, twenty coaches drove off. When five or ten minutes had elapsed after the departure of the last coach, full of scrubbed, smiling, waving language students I began to feel little surges of panic. How could I have missed them? I went back inside the hull of the boat, hoping to see the jewel of the Crown Coaches fleet with its bonnet up, steam hissing from the engine. But no. All that was left was a steady procession of cars, patiently waiting to be allowed off the ship.

This was all very sobering. I was back to earth with a jolt. I started thinking on my feet. My bag was still on the coach. Inside it was all my Belgian currency. I checked my pockets for sterling but even before I could count the miserable pile of coins, I was hit by a series of horrible flashbacks starring me handing over high-denomination notes to grateful bar staff and Duty Free till personnel. I was skint. I was going to have to hitch to Bruges. I couldn't even remember the name of the hotel. I made my way towards the tall mesh exit gates, passing an electricity station on my way. S.E.B. Southern Electricity Board. Danger. High Voltage. Shit. I was back in England.

As it began to dawn on me that I had slept an almighty drunken sleep from Dover to Ostend and back to Dover, I began to have visions of my beloved pals from Huyton shrugging their shoulders and picking through the contents of my holdall. I could see Chris 'Jack' Lyttle squeezing the new Lacoste shirt over his robust stomach but, worse, I could see him swiftly reaching the conclusion that they should spend my money on a memorable wake because it's what I would've wanted.

I phoned my mum to see if there was any message from Belgium, any address or rendezvous. I didn't expect too cheery a reception, but I wasn't prepared for the hysterics which ensued. When I said, suitably shamefaced, "Hello Mum, it's me", there was an initial silence. My ear was then ruptured by a shrill, terrible scream.

Then silence, then an even louder, more horrible wail. After listening loyally to thirty seconds of my mother shrieking like a mad bat, and with my telephone money about to run out, I tried to get to the point. The conversation went as follows:

"Ma, try and calm down will you. What's up with you?"

Silence. Mad shrieking recommences.

"Stop screaming, will you! Has Chris phoned?"

More wailing, but softer now, more like crying, with certain words becoming discernible.

"Get. Home. Hear? Get. Home. Now."

"Has Chris phoned?"

Chris had phoned. Chris had arrived in the hotel in Ostend and thought he may as well get it over with before he settled down to his pre-bender kip. So he'd got my mother out of bed with the following early-morning call.

"A'right. Glad? Yeah. It's Chrissie Boy. Listen, I don't know how to tell you this so I'll come right out with it. It's your Kevin. He's gone. Fell overboard. He was bevvied, like."

This much I gleaned twenty four hours later, sitting in a brilliant bar in Ostend which was playing 'Dreams Never

End' off the first New Order album. After reversing the charges, I managed to calm my poor mum, convince her that Chris Lyttle was a schizophrenic suffering from paranoid delusions and inverted death wish. I stowed back on board the ferry undetected. An excruciating four-hour passage with no food and chronic dehydration took me back to Belgium, where, amazingly given my terrifying, wild-eyed, unwashed hobo look, I hitched a lift to Bruges. But of course Crown Coaches weren't staying in Bruges. Too chic. Too expensive. Back to Ostend. Imagine my ineffable joy when, eventually, I located Jack Lyttle outside a bar, resplendent in a rather tight new Lacoste shirt, buying drinks for all and sundry. I was greeted, I can only imagine, as Our Lord will be next time he pops into Alfie's Bar, Ostend, for a glass of Maes. I said nothing about the shirt and all my cash was exactly where I left it in my bag when I went to get it. Oh! What fun we had over the next couple of days. We drank, we danced badly, we drank, we beat Lockeren (but not Bruges) and we met lots and lots of men from Liverpool. The good ladies of Ostend went untroubled by our presence. Long may the tradition continue.

Kevin Sampson

18

AS Roma v Liverpool
European Cup Final
Rome, 30th May 1984

As soon as Liverpool FC defeated Dynamo Bucharest and secured a place in the final in Rome, a cunningly brilliant plan was devised, worthy of Baldrick of Blackadder fame. Liverpool were to return to the site of their greatest triumph, the Olympic Stadium, where they had first lifted the European Cup in 1977. This was a dream come true. We were to play A.S. Roma on their home ground. Unprecedented, unique, a game you couldn't miss.

As with all these trips, organisation was the key. Many talked a good plan, but few put them into practice. Then a leader emerged from Halewood, a seasoned traveller, a man of his word. He was one of the few hardy souls who had once travelled to Georgia to see Liverpool play Dynamo Tbilisi, one of the best European teams I have had the privilege of seeing at Anfield. Mono, as he was known to his friends, became the organiser. His plan was remarkably simple. Contact a disreputable travel agent, sell him the idea of taking fifty undesirables to Rome for a week at cut-throat prices and wait for the phone to ring.

It is important to remember that these were the days of DIY travel arrangements. The local media ran a few scare stories, that Rome was fully booked around the date of the match. This was due to an unheard of religious festival. Rome, religion, Vatican, festival; it all made perfect sense. There would be "No Vacancy" signs everywhere if you just hopped onto a plane. This was meant to be an inducement to travel on the official tours which seemed ridiculously over priced for a very brief stay in Rome. In comparison, Mono's trip was positively appealing; if a little worryingly cheap. Large bubonic plague carrying rats were smelt, but nothing prepared us for the horrors and hilarity in store.

Our party was about fifty strong and consisted of a group of amiable chaps living on the margins of society known as "The Halewood Chains". Representatives of the inappropriately named "Huyton Baddies" who resembled the Mexican bandidos of spaghetti westerns made up the rest of the contingent, as well as other unattached groups of friends. Our gregarious group of ambassadors pretended to belong to the Genghis Khan school of cultural awareness. Our departure point was the Leatherbottle public house in Halewood, a full five days before the big day. Jaws dropped as our transport to Manchester Airport arrived. It was a 1950's style St Trinians bus and was pretty difficult to start. The curtains had been thickened by decades of smoke and schoolchildren's vomit. It was the bus from an "acid" nightmare. It was going to be a rocky road, you could feel it!

I'm a terrible flyer. I convince myself that every flight is going to be my last. I experience panic attacks and sleep deprivation for several nights before I travel. Imagine my horror when we arrived (safely) in Italy at what I presumed to be Rome Airport, only to see the sign Napoli through the misty windows. Oh no! We'd have to take off and land again. My muscles tensed and I lost myself in an alcoholic haze. When we arrived at Rome Airport, things began to look up, as a relatively modern coach turned up to take us to our seaside paradise on the outskirts of Rome. Mono was toasted. He'd pulled off his own little Italian Job, he was a hero. The toasting was premature. We were travelling for what seemed like hours. Surely Rome wasn't this far from the airport. It wasn't, but Ladispoli was!

Ladispoli was a resort that had seen better days. Like New Brighton without the glamour and lights. And there was the noise, the ceaseless noise. It was out of season and things were being built. Our idyllic destination was a building site. Then there was the Hotel Miramare, a low rent abode run by the Weird Family, generations of them. Of course we were the only guests, in fact we were the only tourists in this excuse for a resort.

Several of my close friends took one look at the facilities on offer and the personal hygiene of the staff, and exited, stage left, for Ostia, the playground for Rome's young, charismatic fun seekers. I decided on selfless solidarity and elected to stay in Dullsville, besides I convinced myself that fun was to be had in such a mind numbingly boring place. My thoughts were prophetic. Our first night out was anything but dull. Groups of ten to fifteen Liverpudlians walking into bars with one loud jukebox and a pin ball machine had a profound effect on the locals. They were stunned into a disbelieving silence. Icy stares welcomed us wherever we ventured, which wasn't far as the town could only boast five bars. Obviously news of our arrival spread around the town, because within half an hour or so the scooter boys had arrived. They were aggressively marking out their territory with ridiculous accelerations. Our presence was presumably an affront to their posturing

51

High Noon at the Bar Internationale

Italian machismo and within minutes the uneasy calm was shattered.

We'd made our HQ in the ironically named Bar Internationale and we were soon surrounded Fort Apache, the Bronx style, by what seemed like the whole town. Scooterboys, Bikers, Teds, Elvis-lookalikes, Italian Casuals, Ultras, Modettes, priests, mothers, fathers, grannies and grandads. The crowd was hostile, but not enough for us to be unduly worried. There must have been about three hundred people milling about the plaza, but only about fifty of these were young braves, intent on "killing the English", the majority had come out of curiosity and to stare at the strange men from foreign shores who had mysteriously selected their unspeakable resort.

The scooter boys gesticulated and waved their fists making cutting actions, but we were unconcerned, laughing at The Elvis-lookalikes from the confines of the bar. This incensed them even more but thankfully Angelo appeared from nowhere, brandishing a gun. Initially we thought, "Oh no, they've got guns", but Angelo was the trendy plainclothed community policeman. He was popular, fashionable and sexy and it soon became apparent that all the girls in the crowd, as well as the grannies and the odd priest fancied him. He could also speak perfect English. We could do business. We asked him to ask the crowd to ask us "to stick around for a while", like in the opening scene of Butch Cassidy and the Sundance Kid, and there would be peace. After all, we had to live together for a week. Angelo pulled it off and peace broke out to cheers from the crowd. In a gesture of reconciliation ·a football match was arranged for later in the week.

The match took on epic proportions. It was the talk of the town. Cheering crowds gathered with all manner of percussion. As you can imagine the phlegmatic Italians were more skilful but what our boys lacked in technique they made up for in passion, and the good old fashioned cry of footballers with limited abilities, "Get stuck into them." The Italians won convincingly of course, but over the last few years or so with the aid of selective amnesia we have convinced ourselves that we won on penalties, just as Liverpool did the next night in Rome.

The Peace Match - the pride of Liverpool and Angelo!

To the Roma fans, victory against Liverpool on their own turf was a foregone conclusion. Bunting and flags adorned most city streets declaring ROMA CAMPIONI 1984 - not "Championi" as some English fans wrongly sang it! Liverpool were meant to be the sacrificial "Christians", to be devoured at the Colosseum in full view of the baying mob. When the two teams came onto the pitch I've never heard a noise like it. It was beyond description. Primeval, and loud. Louder than anything I've heard before or since and the stadium didn't even have a roof. The roar must have been reminiscent of the tumult that welcomed the arrival of the gladiators into the Colosseum. I momentarily thought of all those contests, and now we were in the lions' den, there to be gorged, or so the script read. But it didn't work out like that and within minutes of Liverpool being presented with the trophy

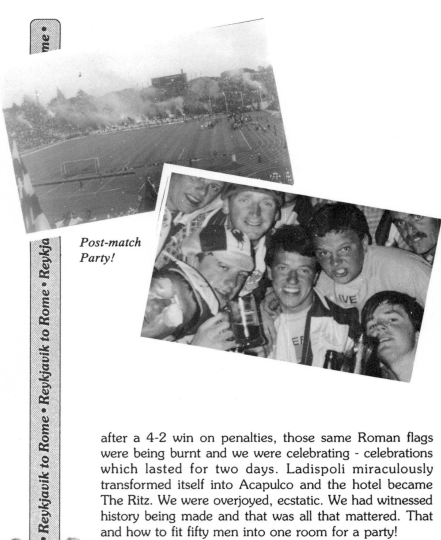

*Post-match
Party!*

after a 4-2 win on penalties, those same Roman flags were being burnt and we were celebrating - celebrations which lasted for two days. Ladispoli miraculously transformed itself into Acapulco and the hotel became The Ritz. We were overjoyed, ecstatic. We had witnessed history being made and that was all that mattered. That and how to fit fifty men into one room for a party!

PS. Several years later refugees from Russia and the former Yugoslavia appeared in a documentary complaining about being dumped by the Italian authorities in a resort outside Rome. The name of the resort was Ladispoli.

Peter Hooton

19

A missed chance or I wasn't there

Rome, Paris, Munich, Belgrade, Moscow....Liverpool were there. I wasn't. Sorry.

When I'm with a couple of mates watching old football videos or just talking drunken nonsense in the pub I'd love to be able to throw in stories about the laugh I had on the Reds pre-season tour to Belgium, or the glorious European Cup final night in Paris, but I wasn't there. Sorry.

I haven't even got any good excuses. At least the fans who support Grimsby or Hartlepool can sleep soundly in their beds at night because they've never had the opportunity to follow their team on to the continent. But me, I had the opportunity to follow the team I've supported all my life and witness at first hand some of the greatest nights in British club football and I blew it. I hit the bar, I blazed the ball wide of a gaping goal, I missed my chance. Sorry.

I wish I had a good excuse but I haven't. There were times when I was too young, or I didn't have the money, but mainly I was just too lazy, I'd miss my girlfriend, and my Mum had scared me off with tales of dodgy foreign food.

I remember when I was about 15 my mate Joey tried to convince me to go to see Liverpool's first big European final in Rome but I was never really interested. (We'd already been in trouble together before when as 11 year olds we'd bunked off one afternoon to watch Liverpool win the League at Wolverhampton). From what I remember the fare was about £50, which I didn't have, and I didn't really fancy being stuck on a train for about a week with loads of sweaty, beery men. Even at that age I wasn't very adventurous. I liked my bed and my Mum's food. I watched the final on the telly and went to bed. Joey came back to school the followings, week looking like death.

But come to think of it there was one occasion when I had a genuine excuse. I was in the middle of my final year exams at University when Liverpool played AS Roma at the Olympic Stadium in the European Cup Final. I had an exam the next morning and I needed to be bright and alert, so I sort of set myself some rules. I was going to stay at home right up until the kick off, I wasn't going to drink, and I was going to go to bed early. I managed to do a bit of revision up until about half an hour before the kick off and then I decided to watch the match at a mate's house. (There were always too many of my sisters in our house). My mate had a drink, so I had a few and the match flew by. Phil Neal scored for us before they pulled it back. All thoughts of the forthcoming exam were lost in the horrible tension. Extra time - bang goes the early night. More tension. "I hope it doesn't go to penalties. There's no way we'll win on pens." (As every schoolboy knows the continentals are great at penalties and free kicks, we are crap.) It goes to penalties. I need another drink.

Incredibly we win. I do a little celebratory dance around the room. I have another drink.

Eventually I go home and go to bed but I'm so hyped up its virtually impossible to sleep. It doesn't matter though because I'm on such a high that I sail through the exam.

I wish I could say that I was there. I wasn't But it was still one of the best nights of my life.

Kevin McManus

20

Bayern Munich v Everton
European Cup-Winners Cup
Semi-Final, 1st Leg, 10th April 1985

If you are under forty, the greatest season for an Evertonian has to be 1984-85. Of course there had been great years before - I vividly remember 1966, '68 and '70. Alan Ball is my all-time hero, as he is for most of my friends and contemporaries, but the achievements of 1984-85 and the style in which they were accomplished stand out.

Most Evertonians would pick the home leg of the European Cup Winners Cup semi-final against Bayern Munich as the greatest game and achievement of the season, winning after conceding an early goal. But for me the greatest game has to be the first leg in Munich.

Ever since I had entered adult life, I had dreamed of watching Everton play one of the top teams in Europe in the final stages of a European competition, and they didn't get much bigger than Bayern Munich. This game was my first opportunity.

Our gang of mates had been to most games that season, but as ever, money was tight, so we rooted around for the cheapest way of travelling. We finally sorted out a coach

package, which offered a two-night stay in Munich. It turned out to be the trip from Hell, a Chevy Chase style, National Lampoon wander across Europe. In fact it was the most disorganised European "yomp" since the British Expeditionary Force had shuffled off to France in 1940.

Lacking leadership and organisation we set off from the Albert Pub, opposite Anfield, of all places. It set the tone for the trip, as did the ancient videos of "Carry on Window Cleaner" and "Morecambe and Wise" which were offered as entertainment. We all knew them word perfect by the time we got home.

We had drivers that didn't know the way, no booking on the ferry, no drinks, no food and an on-board toilet that was blocked before we left Liverpool.

We arrived in Munich ten hours late. Worse still it was "pissing down" and we didn't have a coat between us.

Munich city centre was a contrast of architectural styles - gothic, medieval and ultra modern. Although to be honest, the building we found most impressive was the Löwenbrau Brewery.

Our gang of mates split up; half shot straight off to the red light district, while the other half went on a culture-vulture sight-seeing trip. We visited the Cathedral, the famous Beer Hall, the Opera House and the Beer Hall again. Then we went off to the suburbs, to the place that made the biggest impression of all - the town of Dachau, best known for the infamous concentration camp. We were half-cut when we got there, but the immense scale of the place soon sobered us up.

We returned to Munich in a sombre mood, but the excitement and colour of enthusiastic fans travelling to the Olympic Stadium soon lightened our spirits. This is what we had come here for. Whichever team you support, there is nothing like the feeling generated by a big night game. Whether it's Rochdale or Milan, the feeling is the same. My heart was pounding as we approached the stadium, elated to run into gangs of mates. The Bayern fans were friendly and we exchanged banter in pigeon-German and English. This was worth going off sick from work, getting nasty letters from the bank, missing out on a Majorcan holiday and the silent treatment from wives and girlfriends.

When the "Rat" led the blue shirts out onto the pitch that night, I cried. When I think about it eleven years later, I still fill up. Just as some people cry when they see a sentimental film, when I think of the blue shirts that night (and it's always the shirt, never the player), that's the way I feel.

That night, Everton achieved a magnificent draw (football cliché!) That was the launch pad for a remarkable return to Goodison Palace - the home of football.

Paul Michael Fillis.

21

Memories of Munich

During the early months of 1985 I had started my first job and was learning to drive. Every spare penny was put aside to save for a car as I strived to join the adult world.....

Then suddenly Everton had reached the semi-final of the Cup Winners Cup.

The Olympic Stadium, with its weird roof. 1974 World Cup. Augenthaler, Matthäus, Lerby and Rummenigge. One step from glory. I had to go.

Rip-off tours; one day in Munich. Idiots kissing the runway. Three thousand Evertonians, drinking, chanting, here we go-ing Blues.

Breathtaking stadium. No Andy Gray, no Kevin Sheedy. Backs to the wall; break-aways; more intense pressure. Battling finish. 0-0. Fans on the pitch; mad hairy police. dogs.

Rotterdam, here we come!

Phil Redmond

22

Everton v Bayern Munich
European Cup-Winners Cup Semi-final
2nd Leg 24th April 1985

The support for Everton that night was truly phenomenal. There was just a buzz around the whole of the ground. It might sound like a cliché, but the atmosphere that night was electric. Of course, Bayern scored first and at half-time we found ourselves losing. But the second half saw a complete turnaround. Andy Gray equalised, Graeme Sharp made it 2-1 and then came that most wonderful of goals by Trevor Steven. It was a one-to-one situation with their goalkeeper. Steven scored and the roof came off Goodison. It was truly unbelievable. Everyone was just hugging each other and it certainly was an occasion I'll remember for the rest of my life.

These days I can't get to all Everton's matches because I'm often away playing snooker but I watch them as much as possible and one of these days I'm hoping to see my young son Josh playing for them. He's two years old and always wearing the Everton kit Duncan Ferguson has bought him. Duncan is a good fellow and young Josh couldn't have a better mentor.

John Parrott

23

Goodison Glory

The most memorable match that I have seen is the Everton versus Bayern Munich European Cup-Winners' Cup match played at Goodison Park in 1985. Played on a Spring evening in front of a capacity crowd of over 50,000 the atmosphere was electric.

Both teams were evenly matched for most of the first half and then a shocked crowd saw the German team score just before half-time. When the teams re-appeared for the second half the noise was deafening. The Gwladys Street Choir was in full voice and then the "Blues" scored through Andy Gray! - it was one apiece and the crowd was urging their team on. In a crescendo of noise Everton made it 2-1 and then added a further goal. Andy Gray was convinced that the Gwladys Street crowd had "sucked" the ball into the net for the goals!

The whole team went off to a standing ovation at the final whistle, having beaten one of the finest teams in Europe, and went on to win the competition by beating Rapid Vienna in the final. It was all a far cry from the days when I used to play truant from St. Edward's College to watch the "Blues" playing on Wednesday afternoons in the 1940s for nine old pence!

Pat Kielty

24

Everton v Rapid Vienna
UEFA Cup Final
1985, Rotterdam, 15th May 1985

My story is about following Everton to the UEFA Cup Final in Rotterdam. I along with a gang of Evertonian friends from the Farmers Arms pub in Clubmoor left by coach for Rotterdam on the Monday evening, returning the following Saturday after Everton had played Manchester United at Wembley.

We arrived at Ostend on Tuesday afternoon and booked into our hotel from which we would travel to Rotterdam for the Final. Anyway, you can imagine we had a right good time and there were many hilarious situations that we found ourselves in, but the one that sticks out in my mind is the morning after we had won the Cup.

We were leaving Ostend, bound for Wembley. It was a beautiful morning. The sun was shining and we'd won the Cup. Everyone on the coach was drunk with success and happiness. The coach doors and windows were open and flags and banners were flying from the roof. We were giving Everton flags, hats and rosettes to Belgian kids. Everyone was singing to our tape on the coach - the song that Everton had swept all aside to, "Here we go!"

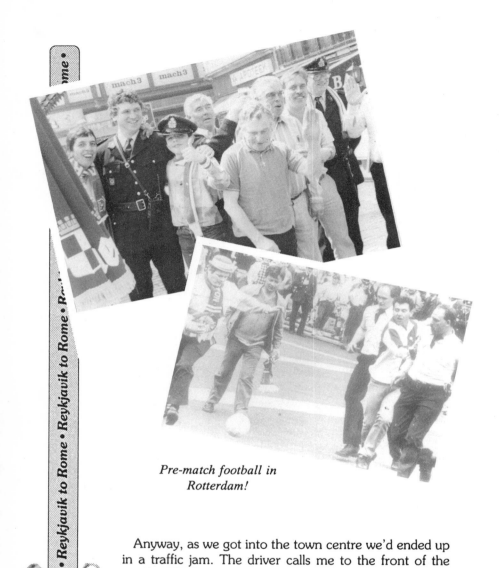

Pre-match football in Rotterdam!

Anyway, as we got into the town centre we'd ended up in a traffic jam. The driver calls me to the front of the coach and tells me we were along side a funeral procession. I looked out and in front of us was a hearse. The coffin was draped in the Belgian flag and people all in black were crying in the funeral cars. I took the mike and asked for a show of respect, which was given.

After half an hour or so we were still crawling behind the funeral cars. We started to sing again and the driver said we could sing if we kept it low. So we started off again, very low key, but after a few minutes someone started, "There he goes, there he goes, there he goes" and the whole coach joined in, full blast, scarves and banners flying. Without meaning to be disrespectful, it was one of the funniest sights you could ever see: funeral cars followed by a coachload of overjoyed Evertonians! If a film had been made of it, I'm sure it would have been a classic.

Anton Garvey

25

Juventus v Liverpool
European Cup Final
Brussels, 29th May 1985

Liverpool and Juventus supporters on the day before the match.

It might have been different.

• Reykjavik to Rome • Reykjavik to Rome • Reykjavik to Rome • Reykjavik to Rome •

26

Blue Spanish Eyes

In November 1988, I found myself on holiday in Spain, visiting my friend John, who was teaching English in Bergarra, a small town in the Basque region. On my first night John introduced me to one of his pupils, Ped, who was wearing an Everton shirt and whose limited English included alarmingly large chunks of the television commentary for Everton's European Cup triumph in Rotterdam. A completely useless party trick, but needless to say, I was mightily impressed.

Ped told me his favourite player was "Don Von Huey", which, drunk as I was, I translated to "Van den Hauwe", a left back best described as enthusiastic, (hem, hem). Try as I might I could not persuade Ped that our doughty hero's name was actually pronounced "Hong Kong Fooey", an incompetent Kung Fu mutt. To me the similarities were boundless, but quite rightly, Ped would have none of it.

Ped told us that he could get tickets for the forthcoming local derby and before the night degenerated completely, vino-fuelled plans were afoot. The match was between Real Sociedad and Athletico Bilbao and was being played at Sociedad's stadium in the rather exclusive San Sebastian

right

• *Reykjavik to Rome* • *Reykjavik to Rome* • *Reykjavik to Rome* • *Reykjavik to Rome* •

• *Reykjavik to Rome* • *Reykjavik to Rome* • *Reykjavik to Rome* • *Reykjavik to Rome* •

• *Reykjavik to Rome* • *Reykjavik to Rome* • *Reykjavik to Rome* • *Reykjavik to Rome* •

• *Reykjavik to Rome* • *Reykjavik to Rome* • *Reykjavik to Rome* • *Reykjavik to Rome* •

• *Reykjavik to Rome* • *Reykjavik to Rome* • *Reykjavik to Rome* • *Reykjavik to Rome* •

• *Reykjavik to Rome* • *Reykjavik to Rome* • *Reykjavik to Rome* • *Reykjavik to Rome* •

• *Reykjavik to Rome* • *Reykjavik to Rome* • *Reykjavik to Rome* • *Reykjavik to Rome* •

• *Reykjavik to Rome* • *Reykjavik to Rome* • *Reykjavik to Rome* • *Reykjavik to Rome* •

• *Reykjavik to Rome* • *Reykjavik to Rome* • *Reykjavik to Rome* • *Reykjavik to Rome* •

resort. This picturesque bay had traditionally served as a retreat for Spanish royalty, but given the threat of Basque Separatist terrorism, there was more chance of seeing Juan Carlos at a Butlin's adult weekend.

Our small party arrived early in the afternoon, giving us plenty of time for drunken merriment before the evening kick-off. In most of the bars and on some streets there were elaborately painted murals in honour of ETA, the PLO and the IRA. This probably explained why San Sebastian is one Spanish resort which is a Union-Jack-Boxer-Shorts Free-Zone.

On the way to the ground we came across two buses and several cars that were smouldering away gently, having been hijacked, abandoned and then set alight. Ped assured us that this was nothing more than "hi jinx" typical of the occasion. My, how we laughed! The fact that the place was crawling with heavily armed police with itchy fingers was also of no concern. However, when a passing car backfired, I nearly fainted and decided that I would always be more Wolfie Smith than Che Guevara.

Once inside the ground the only dilemma was in deciding which team to support. As an Evertonian, this was not easy. Sociedad were managed by John Toshack, ex-Red, (Yah boo sucks!). On the other hand Bilbao were under Howard Kendall, ex-Blue, (Hurrah!). However, while Bilbao had red in their kit, Sociedad played in blue and white........the best I could hope for was an honourable draw.

In the end it didn't matter, because the match was so grim I can't even remember the score. What I do remember is the massive sense of betrayal I felt . That Senor Kendall had left us for this! For this! Still, as they say, that's another story.

Sean P Casey

70

27

Everton v Feyenoord

European Cup-Winners Cup,
2nd Round, 1st Leg 19th October 1995

It was only at the last minute that I found I had an opportunity to go to this match. I was surprised that it was not all-ticket and that there were no queues at the turnstiles. It was particularly surprising because it was our first European campaign for ten years and the opposition were one of several Dutch clubs to have performed well in European competitions. Many things had changed since previous European matches. The fixture itself was being played on a Thursday night, unheard of in the days before television's dominance.

About fifteen minutes before kick-off, a large number of Feyenoord supporters were allowed to join us in the Main Stand, which is usually reserved for home fans only. The Dutch had brought over a large following. There was to be no fighting between the two sets of supporters here, in fact, no contact of any kind.

A former Dutch international player, John de Wolf appeared in the stand. He was playing for Wolverhampton Wanderers at the time, or rather refusing to play for their reserves. He was immediately recognised by his long blond hair, headband and beard. A lot of Feyenoord supporters sought his autograph and photo opportunities. We did our best to ignore all this.

The clubs were obviously working hard at European integration. A Dutch-speaking announcer shared tannoy duties with Everton's. He was also allowed to play some Euro-pap and what seemed to be the Feyenoord theme tune. A group of local schoolchildren were dressed up in Dutch costume and paraded a message of welcome or friendship on the pitch. This received some appreciation, although the Feyenoord supporters were later to respond with insulting chants in perfect English.

The game itself was the very entertaining type of goalless draw. We played three central defenders and, although relatively unfamiliar with the formation, we looked solid and produced some good controlled movements. We created several chances but with certain key players unavailable, we could not quite score. Feyenoord had their moments and displayed excellent technique but were probably more content with not conceding a goal. Even a Ronald Koeman freekick came to nothing in spite of elaborate preparations.

It was a memorable occasion for me, and I wished I had had more chances to see European matches.

David Stoker

28

The Final Whistle

The doctor diagnosed M.S. Basically what it meant was that my body was falling apart at an unpredictable rate. Reluctantly, I had to give up work, so, feeling sorry for myself at home, I fought off depression by entering every competition that I could. I nearly fell off the couch when I saw my name in the Football Echo; I had won a coach trip to Spain to see Real Sociedad against Barcelona. It was February '90. Liverpool supporters had been banned from Europe and John Aldridge was playing in the Spanish League for Real Sociedad. I just managed to scrape a few bob together and with passport renewed, I took up my seat. With my condition deteriorating, I had decided then that this would be my final game. We reached Dover and safely crossed the Channel. There isn't much to see in Northern France, so with the coach chewing up the motorway and night-time falling I got me head down....

....Years of football rolled over in my head. We lived off Oakfield Road, so I grew up with the clatter and songs from the Kop; passing footsteps taking away the smell of hot dogs, lying in bed of a night listening to the traffic as the glow of car headlights danced around

my bedroom window. *Terry Venables, Derek Dougan and John Hollins lay in a fan on the bedroom cabinet, waiting to be stuck in a glossy album. There were always a couple of players you could never get, like Charlie Cooke and Colin Suggett. One morning, there was a determined knock at the door. Norman Jarvis hated his name which didn't really matter 'cos everyone called him Chip-Pan anyway.*

"You could fry an egg on that lad's head", - me Nan would say. Me Nan never gave him enough credit - you could fry a full English breakfast on Chip-Pan's head. His Ma used to throw him out to school early so he'd come round to our's to bum a bacon butty. With his stubby nailbitten fingers he removed the lazzy band from his wad of Soccer Stars and flipped them from one hand to the other. Our eyes were sharply focussed, "Got, Got, Got, Got, Got,"

"I've got Charlie Cooke twice, Ally!". After careful negotiation, the Chelsea striker was transferred for a crust of toast, and gratefully gummed in between Peter Bonetti and John Dempsey.

Chip-Pan started collecting those 'heavy duty' cardboard cards. While the shopkeeper had her fingers in a jar of Uncle Joe's, Chip-Pan emptied the cornershop. The massive pockets of his green Parka seemed purpose built for the operation. You seemed to get two Frank Caspers in every pack and a shattered piece of pink chewy that tasted like coal-tar soap. It was the only soap Chip-Pan ever saw. Each card had a joke on the back. If the joke didn't make you sick then the chewy would. The cards tasted better than the chewy and I don't know one person who managed to blow bubbles with it although Chip-Pan nearly collapsed a lung trying. Me Nan had her own prognosis: "Yer guts'll stick together,lad!"

Me and Chip-Pan sagged school and hung around the ground waiting for players. Kit bag in hand, Tommy Smith walked out on to Annie Road with Alec Lindsay. I collared them for an autograph with a sparkling new Parker pen that me Nan bought me. The veins in Tommy's hands swelled as he scribbled his name on a red 'City of Liverpool' exercise book. Alec didn't get the chance; the pen fell from Tommy's grasp. He made an attempt to catch it but seemed to go for it in weekly instalments. My Parker pen rattled its way down the grid. Tommy put his hand in his pocket, and as he walked off he threw a 10p coin over;

"Buy a new one lad".

When I got home me Nan battered me, "The bloody minge bag," she said. The old woman died hating Tommy Smith.

My first official visit to Anfield was unofficial - a gang of us bunked in. There's only one thing worse than watching Bury and that's watching Bury Reserves. A copper ended the misery by giving us a chase. Chip-Pan got over the fence safely but I found the red gate too much. A scuffed 'slip-on' shoe fell as I was dangling from the railings. A bearded copper then grabbed me:

"I'm going to see your father!"

This copper knows me old man? I didn't even know him myself! He was a seaman. "The other side of the world's too close for him", me Nan used to say. Anyway, this copper started speaking into his walkie-talkie: the thing wasn't even turned on. Chip-Pan came back - he's another lyin' bastard, "Our kid's got an 'ole in' is 'eart. And I've...and I've only got one lung!" We got away with a boot up the arse.

A sanction inflicted soon after marriage is the 'away games ban'. My wife threatened to leave if I went to another away match. So I stopped going - and we started winning. Because of the wife's sanction we not only had a chance of the 'Double', we near had a brand new pine kitchen, with the money we'd saved. All we needed were a couple of points off Chelsea to win the League. "You go and you know they'll only lose" she'd say. On the bakery floor, a buzz had grown all week. It was Spring '86, the week before the first Merseyside F.A. Cup Final. That Saturday morning, as I came home off nights, red scarves were waving heading for the Capital. As I opened the front door, she shouted downstairs: "It's lovely and warm up here, love!" "Just goin' out to buy a paper", I shouted. Forgot to tell her I was goin' to Stamford Bridge to get it. I got home drunk in the early hours.

The first thing to hit me was a piece of knotty pine, then a tin of gloss varnish; she turned gangster on me, with a Black'n'Decker in her hands....

....With a back as stiff as an ironing-board and a tongue that felt like a mattress in the roof of my mouth, I was coming out of a drowsy haze and amongst the chatter I could hear the rhythm of the engine. The fella opposite kept me informed; "Bet you're glad you slept through France aren't yer, lad? - nearly a fiver for a fartin' carton of chips. Seventy pence a chip, I made it." The enquiry into the price of Parisian potatoes was interrupted by the sight of the sun-splashed Med. 'The Aldo Express' had reached the Costa Brava. We checked in at our hotel in Lloret de Mar. It was Carnival Weekend, so we spent the first night getting into the spirit, drinking.

The next morning, it was match day. Our coach was making its way down the white avenidas of Barcelona. At that time the city was receiving a face-lift. We spent some time looking around the Olympic site before making our way to Barcelona's Nou Camp Stadium.

Real Sociedad come from the Basque city of San Sebastian. Just for that game and with John Aldridge in their strikeforce, we obviously shouted for them. Because Aldo has a Bachelors L.P., Jack Chariton made him a full international; so the boys from Lime Street's 'Yankee Bar' held the Irish flag aloft. We had seats high above the half-way line and saw Barcelona go into a two goal lead. With Laudrup and Koeman in their ranks the home team walked off at half-time with "Barca! Barca!", ringing in our ears. In the second-half our local lad netted twice and would have got a hat-trick but for a dodgy offside decision. Aldo was given a great reception by us; after a performance like that, he deserved it. We left the Nou Camp with no doubt who we were and where we had come from - I swallowed hard, as I left the Stadium.

The next morning was Sunday: the highlight of Carnival Weekend. Time for a sunny Catalonian Festival. To the sound of the band, the streets of Lloret were paraded by adults and children colourfully dressed as soldiers, clowns and jesters. At dinnertime we had a pint in the hotel. During this it was mentioned that the local team, Lloret, were playing Europa in the Spanish Third Division. This was a local derby and at that time both teams were locked at the top of the League.

The whole coach had turned up for the 3 o'clock kick off. After paying about a fiver, the ninety of us were escorted to the visitors' enclosure; a little paddock at the side of the pitch. It would've been too easy to support the home team so we shouted for the visitors. Lloret had never sold so much San Miguel and the till rattled on to the sound of: "Europa! Europa!"

Europa kicked off in their navy blue strip, spurred on by our waving red scarves. Aldo's Irish Flag rippled green, white and orange in a sunny breeze. Lloret, in paler blue, were constantly booed. Then Europa took the lead and our red and white mob got behind them;

"Europa! Europa!"

Just after half-time Lloret equalised. Then, a podgy Europa substitute warmed up along the touch-line. Waving a pen, one of the boys from the Yankee Bar spoke to him: "Sign me shirt, super striker!"

The Europa sub obliged, scrawling on the back of a red shirt. A moment later our section was chanting; "Pedro! Pedro!" With scores level and time running out, the baldy Europa trainer gave in to our pleas and Pedro took to the field, every touch given frantic applause; "Pedro! Pedro!" The row we were making inspired Europa. The ball was played up front and bobbled around the box. Pedro gave it the 'wellie', nearly bursting the net. Pedro's pals celebrated. An army of Liverpool supporters trampled on to the pitch. Sanity returned and the game continued with a member of 'The Policia' assigned to us.

In the Police canteen that morning, this copper thought he'd drawn a long enough straw avoiding the Carnival crowds, the Bank Holiday traffic and pushin' a trolley round the 'El Asda' with the missus; instead he'd got English football supporters! In the dying seconds Europa scored again. Ecstatic players ran over to us, Latin fists waving and white teeth gleaming. Fuelled by thoughts of promotion and The Armada, King Canute of the constabulary bravely stood his ground, with arms raised. "Retrocedan! Retrocedan! Back, back! Go back!"

The English crew sailed past; a blue peaked hat fell to the grass. King Canute was overthrown. The match was then played out, and as the referee 'blew up' to end the rout, the red and white canter returned to the pitch. Pedro and company were mobbed and carried around the pitch. Along with Spanish sweat, tears of joy rolled down Pedro's face.

The next morning we left sunny Spain behind, heading home for the wind and rain. Whatever way the wind blows, I'm always glad to get home. I was tired and skint as I crossed back on the ferry. I couldn't even afford a drink from the duty-free. Instead I brought something else home with me: Human Spirit, something that you can't buy in a bottle. My prime may be restricted, but there are some who don't reach theirs. We're still in the game and the crowd is on our side. It's only the first half; who knows what the second will bring. So we'll keep playing till **the Final Whistle.**

Ian Halliwell

Acknowledgements

Special thanks to:

Alan Adlington, Danny Burns, Paul Burton, Franny Ferris, Michael Fillis, Billy Flanagan, Anton Garvey, Peter Hooton, Tony McClellan and Steve Monaghan for their generous contribution of photographs and memorabilia.

The photographs on pages 11, 13, 59 and 64 (top) copyright of Liverpool Daily Post and Echo.

• Reykjavik to Rome • Reykjavik to Rome • Reykjavik to Rome • Reykjavik to Rome •

• Reykjavik to Rome • Reykjavik to Rome • Reykjavik to Rome • Reykjavik to Rome •